MY BUMPS
HAVE A PURPOSE

DR. MELANIE P. MANOR

MY BUMPS HAVE A PURPOSE!

ARTIST: KRIS WILSON

HE IS WITH US ALL THE TIME!
Deuteronomy 31:6

By Dr. Melanie P. Maxor

FREE WOMEN OF GOD MINISTRIES

Presents

MY BUMPS HAVE A PURPOSE

DR. MELANIE P. MANOR

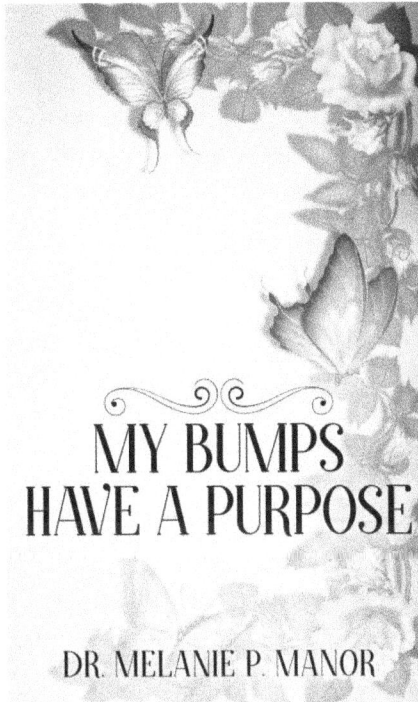

HE IS WITH US ALL THE TIME

Deuteronomy 31:6 (AMP)

"Be Strong and Courageous. Do not be afraid or tremble in dread before them, for it is the Lord your God who goes with you. He will not fail you or abandon you."

By Dr. Melanie P. Manor

3

Published by Aspiring Knowledge, Inc, LLC. Arlington, Texas 76011 USA

Email Address: mybumpshaveapurpose@gmail.com

Book design copyright© 2019.   All rights reserved.
Cover design by BetiBup33
Interior design by Dr. Melanie P. Manor

Published in the United States of America
ISBN: 978-0-578-50479-7
1. Non-Fiction 2. Family Life

To order additional copies of this book, send a request to the email below:

Dr. Melanie P. Manor
Mybumpshaveapurpose@gmail.com
81290

DEDICATIONS

I want to thank GOD for His grace, mercy, and goodness that He bestowed upon me. Also, for walking with me through the good and the bad times of my life. I also want to thank God for preparing and equipping me as I went through each bump. He walked with me through it all, even when I turned my back on Him, He was still walking with me.

I dedicate this book to all the women that have gone through something and think life hasn't been great or fair for them. You're here to tell of God's goodness in your life. It's liberating and healing. You're built for this and with God's strength, you can accomplish anything. I pray you to resign from trying to run your life today and turn it over to God.

Dear GOD,

OK, I resign. I've been trying to run the world and probably the universe, at least the things I thought I controlled and I'm fed up doing this job, it's too much. I've never been a quitter, but I quit. Please take the job back. I know you won't do things the way I would've done it and I'm Ok with that, but I'm sure you will do a much better job. Please take it back! I need to sleep at night and I want to sit back and watch the great things you're going to do in my life.

I know that You're in charge and that You'll take care of things. There will be days when I want to take control but don't let me, remind me so I don't have to cry again. You're PERFECT and You know me better than I know myself! You may not do it exactly when I want it, but you're always right on time. Take this as my final resignation. Thank you and I love you, Lord!

Dr. Mel

This book allows you to see your strength and it also allows you to see that you can overcome anything with the help of the Lord. You're not an accident; your bumps also have a purpose for you and what you are to do in this world. God bless you and thank you for reading this book.

ACKNOWLEDGEMENT

I want to recognize all those that assisted me in perfecting this book, all my friends, pastors and those that gave their support from inception. I thank GOD for the opportunity to experience all the things I have in life thus far and I'm honored to experience the newness of GOD now. I thank Him for the strength and fortitude He has given me to complete this work. Thank You, Jesus!

Special recognition goes to my husband, Minister Dr. Vincent D. Manor I, who has been a rock to me and extremely encouraging while I'm telling my story. Honey, you are the greatest version of what GOD calls a "True Man of GOD", thank you.

These journeys happened years ago but I want to thank those that have understood that change can happen in a person and GOD can work with you if you work with Him. My love is for helping the people of God change. Also, to be empowered by what GOD has given them. This has inspired me to tell my story. Thank you all for listening to me in sunday school, in the pulpit, at work, and in the mission field. You are truly a GOD given inspiration.

I would like to recognize my family, particularly my mom who is the strongest woman I know. I used to think she was a super-hero because she made life so easy for me even though she was going through. GOD sustained me through all the bumps, bruises, mistakes, and even the good times in my past and especially my future.

To those that are in great support of my mission to serve God, your enthusiasm, your trust in me and the advice given at times helped me tell this story to help others. Thank you for being part of GOD's training ground and being part of His Kingdom experience.

TABLE OF CONTENTS

Forward 8
Introduction.. 10
A Word from the Author 11
About the Author 12
Lonely But Not Alone 13
Young Parents 23
Athletics and Education 30
My Strength Was Their Problem (The Violators)..... 37
7 Pregnancies and No Births 44
Failed Relationships 48
Living a Contrary Lifestyle – The Revelation 52
Running From Love 57
Accepting my Calling with God Again 62
My Kingdom Adventure 67
Your Declaration to God 74
My Spiritual Tool Kit 75

      You Are What You Eat 81

      Resigning from Doing Cods Job 83
      God Loves Order 85
      Have God Faith 88
      Whom am I in Christ? 90
      Living & Applying the Word 92
      Sowing 94
      Nurture the Seed 96

FOREWORD

Dr. Mel,

ME/ Living, Learning and Loving
Making Everything Legitimate

John 8:32
"And ye, shall know the truth and the truth you know shall make you free."

Knowing truth and becoming one with truth is what you'll find in the pages as you walk through this life long experience. This book shows you the truth about struggle, the stains and finally supernatural salvation, the survival sets one up for success. In the old testament God chooses individuals to personify grace like Mephibosheth, he personified the grace of God like no other. He was hurt, crippled and should have been discarded but destiny said NO.

Dr. Mel now knows truth and it has set her free i.e. unrestricted, unrestrained and able to move about at will and not as a slave but a free person indeed.

James writes in chapter 1:2 "**Count it all Joy**".   This is what I see in this young lady's life.

Consider	In	Always	Just
Our	Triumphant	Loving	Over
Ugliness		Life (Because I'm Over it!)	You! (Hurt, etc.)
Necessary			
Today			

Thank you, my friend for sharing your story of His/Story which is His history in you.   I know many will find truth and will experience being free.

Your Friend,

Dr. Charles Kent

Dr. Charles Kent
CEO Joseph Outreach Foundation Inc.

MY BUMPS

This is a reminder that you too can make it!

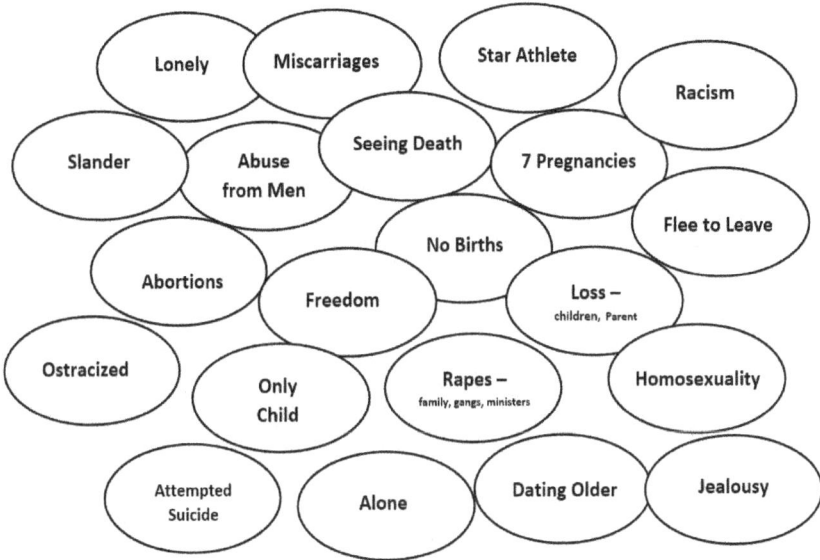

Lonely
Miscarriages
Star Athlete
Racism
Slander
Abuse from Men
Seeing Death
7 Pregnancies
Flee to Leave
No Births
Abortions
Freedom
Loss – children, Parent
Ostracized
Only Child
Rapes – family, gangs, ministers
Homosexuality
Attempted Suicide
Alone
Dating Older
Jealousy

If I survived it, YOU CAN TOO!

INTRODUCTION

As a Minister of the word and a sister to many, I knew that my story could one day help a multitude of people that were afraid to share their success as they came out of the darkness. Sometimes we see things as horrific, but there is always an option to come through. We forget that going through makes us tell of God's goodness in our lives when we come out. Our story then shows the world how God had His hand on us all the time.

I never thought I was worthy of His Love because people never told me, even though I come from a family of preachers and scholars of the word, they didn't tell me that God loved me. I don't remember hearing, "YOU ARE AWESOME". We need to hear that, so I'm here to tell you, YOU ARE AWESOME! I promise you God has never LEFT. It's our actions that turn us away from HIM. The good thing about God is HE walks with us even through the bad times.

God's love is so awesome and I'm glad that I'm able to see and receive HIS love freely every day. I experienced some things in my life that some people don't come through successfully, but you don't have to experience them at all. This book is here to minister to your soul and let you know that God is walking with you, accept HIM and choose to walk correctly NOW!

I have read many books, sermons and heard the word. I went to conferences that assisted and helped me get to this point in my life. I went to a play written by my friend, called, "The Struggle is Real", this play touched me to my core. I realized that if I tell the truth about the fight and the triumph, once you accept Christ into your life, I would've been prepared for the battles and realized that He will not leave me nor forsake me. (Duet. 31:6, AMP)

Please enjoy the book and notice the title "*My Bumps Have A Purpose*! Use my experiences as a lesson for you to change your current state/situations and begin to know Him better.

A WORD FROM THE AUTHOR

Jeremiah 29:11 (AMP), *"For I know the plans and thoughts that I have for you, says the Lord, plans for peace and well-being and not for disaster, to give you a future and a hope."* He has plans for us. This is a promise we can stand on. God's Plan is nothing like anything we can think or imagine. I use to wonder why me, but the deeper I got to know God and the more I allowed Him to control my life, I say WHY NOT ME! God's plan is my best plan.

GOD loves us so much HE gave us FREE WILL to decide how, even in the bad times. We've been made (By GOD) to choose the GOOD over BAD but it doesn't always happen that way. I guess the BAD seems more appealing. Let me tell you, friends, the BAD is not all it's cracked up to be.

Choose Ye this path, Jeremiah 6:16 (AMP) states, *"Thus says the Lord, "Stand by the roads and look; ask for the ancient paths, where the good way is; then walk in it, and you will find rest for your souls. But they said, "We will not walk in it!"* This is the dilemma we have today, we are given the path, but the opposite seems more appealing.

Sometimes we're given a warning about the things we're doing; however, we decide that we're going to do them anyway. Even though we chose that path, GOD was still there, it was us who left him, He never left us. Thank GOD for His Grace and His unselfish love. He welcomes us each time we ask to come back.

This book displays the real transparency in my life and walks you through who I was and came to be. I could have taken a different road but the things that happened only defined how great I'm to be on the earth. I'm a conduit for people, my job is to show you how God can and will make a difference in your life if you surrender. I pray that you take a deep look at yourself and then show the world how God really changed your life. Amen!

ABOUT THE AUTHOR
Dr. Melanie P. Manor

Born in New York now resides in Texas. Dr. Melanie P. Manor (aka Dr. Mel) has a wonderful family, which includes a King, Min. Dr. Vincent D. R. Manor I and children; Tarren and Vincent II. Dr. Mel is a proud grandmother and an aunt to many children.

She's a native of New York and participated in athletics for many years which defined her. Her love turned out to be basketball. She was honored in the New York State high school basketball Hall of Fame, with over 2000 career points and over 1000 rebounds in her senior year. She continued her career collegiately in the NCAA ranks.

A crippling knee injury shortened her career for a short time, but she was able to continue her education after being noticed by a coach in Austin, Texas. This began the second phase of her career. Moving to Austin, Texas allowed her to finish her degree at Huston-Tillotson University in Austin, where she finished her basketball career and graduated with a Bachelor of Science Degree in Computer Technology in 1995. She later received her Honorary Doctorate of Humane Letters from Agape Bible College in North Carolina in 2010.

In 1997, she moved to Dallas to work as a Corporate Leadership Trainer and began coaching girls' basketball, volleyball, and track at Shady Grove Christian Academy. She imparted life skills and spiritual counseling for her players, this is where her ministry began. She started to recognize that training was the talent that GOD gave her. Now in ministry she ministers to the multitudes any chance she gets and uses the talent GOD gave her.

Lonely But Not Alone
Chapter 1

"Haven't I commanded you: Be strong and courageous? Do not be afraid or discouraged, for the Lord your God is with you wherever you go."
Joshua 1:9 (CSB)

Loneliness

What does the bible say about Loneliness? God was even aware that loneliness was not good for man. He was so aware of it that He gave Adam a helpmate. He gave Adam the power to name the animals and foul of the air. He recognized then that loneliness and our need for human interaction with living things was needed.

Everyone experiences seasons of isolation for one reason or another but soon realize there is something missing. Usually, we overcome loneliness by meeting new friends, entering new social circles, or taking some other action that reengages us with people.

How does a young child do this? I was just a child born to young parents and wondering, why am I here in this world alone? I couldn't understand why I didn't have any siblings. I often wanted to ask my Mom and Dad why, but I never did. As I got older, I realized my mom couldn't have any other children, so I was her little lone blessing. Today, we have the best relationship ever, but I didn't see that back then.

Some see loneliness as a negative because society has made us think that being alone is not a good thing. But you're never alone because God is with you all the time.

Loneliness, con't

Now that I'm all grown up, being alone wasn't so bad, once I realized that I wasn't alone at all. God was walking with me all the time and would take care of my every need.

The bible says this about loneliness:

He is the friend who *"stays closer than a brother"* (Proverbs 18:24.5 CSB), *"no one has greater love (nor stronger commitment) than to lay down his own life for his friends"* (John 15:13 AMP), *and who has promised to be with us always (remaining with you perpetually – regardless of circumstances, and on every occasion, even until the end of the age* (Matthew 28:20.5 AMP).

Let's take comfort in that and shout **VICTORY!** You're not alone. *"Friends may fail you; they may come and go but He is with you to the end. Thank you, Jesus, oh how gracious He is with us."*

We should all embrace loneliness at times, this is a time of reflection and worship and it's also a time to listen for that sweet voice of reason (Which is God). I say the voice of reason because the other voice will creep in also.

That voice tells you why you're alone and that you're not worthy to be with others, this can happen to children as well as adults. Don't get it twisted, no one is safe from the enemy's tricks, but you're PROTECTED and SAFE if you're in tune to hear the voice of GOD. *Who are you listening to?*

Creative Imagination

Children tend to have a very creative imagination, especially if they are left alone to exercise it. I often thought of things to do with the time I spent alone, remember my parents were young and trying to find out who they were also.

I often played in my room with all my stuffed animals or got immersed in a television show (I was lucky to have a TV in my room during my young years). I had a lot of freedom to go outside and to get into a lot of trouble. This included coming in late which resulted in punishment in my room. Being on punishment caused me to gaze out the window to see all the other children playing in the neighborhood, so my mind wondered even more. My imagination ran with me during that time of solitude.

As I grew older and had a bit more freedom, I began to dabble and become curious. This is where the cravings of things began. The enemy will try and give you another taste that isn't so sweet, but you don't know that until the bitterness begins to fester.

Cravings

What is a craving? A craving is, "a powerful desire for something" (Google dictionary), I wasn't yet a teenager and these cravings would begin to cloud my mind *(Main Ingredient Navigating my Destiny, an acronym from the book A Word Fitly Spoken, by Dr. Charles Kent)*.

Cravings, con't

I was curious and wanted to know what else is out there for me. I began hanging out with people older than me and this was when my cravings for additional explorations increased. I decided that I needed something to do with my time. I was about 7 or 8 years old when something starting tugging at me.

I began going to the local park by our school and discovered the game of basketball. I stayed in the park watching the local boys for hours. The game of basketball became a love of mine.

I didn't know how to play the game, but I knew this was a game I was interested in. I watched for hours and sometimes got in trouble for coming in late. There was something about the game that really was interesting to me. It was the action of the game, the accolades and the physical nature of it that intrigued me. I really liked this game and wondered if I could learn to play like the neighborhood boys. I noticed that there were no girls playing but that didn't stop me from wanting to be the best at it.

One of the neighborhood boys noticed me watching each day and finally asked me if I wanted to learn how to play. He started being friendly and then offered to teach me the game. He seemed very nice in the beginning and was nice enough to help me learn. He noticed I didn't look like most young girls (I was pretty developed for my age) and he began taking interest in my development but continued to teach me the game and other things as well. *Beware of false prophets!* Their intentions are not to teach, but to devour.

Once we got passed the sport, he became a little more intimate, but I wasn't aware of what he was doing. He showed me so much attention that it overwhelmed me, I'd even go back for this overwhelming feeling and attention.

Why did I go back? The reason is I didn't get that much attention at home, remember my parents were young also.

Cravings, con't

I searched him out each day because my physical nature was driving me toward the attention given. Even though I was craving attention at times, he began to pay too much attention to me, which then began to overwhelm me.

After seeking him daily and wanting this attention he began taking me to private areas where we could be alone, he then introduced me to intimacy and then a young girl was deflowered.

I was so devasted and confused that I didn't tell anyone about it. I often sat and tried to talk it through in my mind but was unsure of what to say, this is where knowing about prayer would've been a good thing.

As an adult, I can say that this is something a young girl should never have to go through. They don't know how to decipher the emotions they feel after that kind of encounter. I would seek him to get that intimate feeling that I didn't even understand. I had no idea what love was at all, it was a craving a false emotion or feeling, the practical definition is, "a powerful desire for something" (Google dictionary) and it controlled me.

"What are your thoughts about this? Are you going through this? Is your child going through this?"

This craving overpowered me so much that I would miss curfew just to encounter it. Remember, once you give yourself to someone, they feel they have a sense of power and entitlement over you.

I personally didn't give myself to him. I didn't understand what was happening. But he felt he was entitled to have my time and everything about me. What was a young girl to do?

17

Cravings, con't

Things with my parents weren't going well during this time, they were young and trying to exist also in the same space, so it was hard to talk to them about what was happening to me. "Be aware of the cravings you seek, let God's grace and glory be your craving".

Jealousy

I had a lot of freedom because my parents were working most times and spending time with each other. They were also going through some things of their own. They didn't notice what was happening to me. I was an athlete and was very good at it even at a young age, I received many accolades and others (young and old) didn't quite take to that. This is when jealousy begins to creep in.

I remember a family friend telling my dad that they thought I was pregnant, my dad asked me about it and asked me to take his tray to the kitchen. On the tray was an article about teenage pregnancy, this alerted me that my secret was out. I felt so little and Dad sat me down and told me to give him the name of the young man that I had the encounter with. Dad even called his parents to discuss the situation. What an embarrassing moment for me?

After a painful conversation, it was confirmed that this was a false alarm but now it's known that I wasn't a virgin any longer. They still didn't know how long it had been happening. I am now 13 years of age.

Some people are jealous of your freedom and will say what they can about you, our family friend was one of them. Whether it's true or not?

Jealousy, con't

I sometimes think the conversation should've gone a different way because it didn't stop me from seeking the attention or stopping the cravings. I thought I should've gotten that father-daughter talk about why this was not good for me, but that never happened. I was still in the same place, seeking cravings.

Did I wake up yet? Of course not, I was too young to understand I was in trouble and this path, if continued, could derail my life.

Freedom

The Google dictionary states that FREEDOM is the "state of not being imprisoned or enslaved". I read an article by Dr. Art Lindsley at the Institute for Faith Work and Economics, it mentioned that God's definition is that "freedom is not autonomy or doing what you feel like doing without constraints, but freedom involves structure. Really, I was in no way thinking about structure during this time.

"Bonding to Christ allows us to be free to be what we are created to be".

We should be able to move without constraint in the sphere for which God made us, but are we really doing that?

A good example of this would be a bird. It's free only when it can move in the air unhindered. When done correctly, your Freedom should be an option to fly unhindered.

Angela Merkel, the Chancellor of Germany mentions in an article:

"Freedom is the very essence of our economy and society. Without freedom, the human mind is prevented from unleashing its creative force. But what is also clear is that this freedom does not stand alone. It is freedom in responsibility and freedom to exercise responsibility."

Freedom, con't

Freedom isn't always a good thing for someone that's not yet responsible enough to handle it. Freedom can "*Make you or Break you*". I believe it did both for me. I had too much time to get into things, but not enough time to learn or to be taught how to get out of them.

"Freedom is being you without anyone's permission", but is that good? I would say not.

Freedom is what creates soul-ties that we don't need in our lives. A soul-tie is a theory that can be explained and understood by anyone. It's the idea that certain actions can connect you to a person and cause you to bond in a way that is not easily broken (Jetmag.com). This is what happened to me at an early age. Once you're given too much freedom and no guidance, the enemy comes in like a flood and you create soul-ties you didn't want.

As I mentioned earlier, I lost my virginity early because of freedom and once I encountered that feeling, the feeling then became a craving. Once I denied the craving, things began to turn bad. The boyfriend I had then became jealous and decided he was going to take it by force.

There are times in your life when you need to look at yourself. Does that really happen to a young girl not even out of her teens yet? Yes, and it is happening to young girls all over the world now.

The good thing about me was my life kept moving forward even though tragedy hit me, but everyone's not that strong. God was with me all the time. He knew me and what I had to do for Him in the earth. This is where freedom soon cost you when you walk out of the will of God unknowingly. I didn't see that I was getting into deeper trouble; I soon had to find a way out.

"*Your willingness to look at your darkness is what empowers you to change.*" Iyanla Vanzant

Freedom, con't

"Struggle is a never-ending process. Freedom is never really won; you earn it and win it in every generation." Coretta Scott King

I was in search for that freedom that was to liberate me, not freedom that wanted to devour me.

MOMENT OF REFLECTION

LONELY BUT NOT ALONE

Even if people turn on you, friends and family members forsake you, or your circumstances separate you from the people you love, you're never alone. God has said, *"…never will I leave you; never will I forsake you"* (**Hebrews 13:5 NIV**).

1. Do you feel God was and is with you all the time even though you don't or didn't know him?
2. God has a plan for you even though you didn't know your direction at that time in your life.
3. He protected your mind and your heart even though you didn't understand either of them and gave it away freely.

What is GOD saying to you now? What are the plans and thoughts GOD has for you now? DO YOU KNOW? If not, ask him. Take this time to talk to Him that created you.

_____
_____
_____
_____
_____
_____
_____
_____
_____
_____
_____
_____
_____
_____
_____
_____
_____

Young Parents
Chapter 2

Children obey your parents in the Lord, (that is, accept their guidance and discipline as His representatives), for this is right (for obedience teaches wisdom and self-discipline). (Eph. 6:1 AMP)

I believe, despite the opposition my parents faced being young teenagers with a child, that I was given the best parents. We all grew up together. There were good times and there were bad times, the strange thing is that I remember more of the good times than the bad. I'm sure my mom has something different to say about that and if my dad was alive, he would have another story.

My mother was a young woman with a child but had so much fight in her that she was determined to make it in life and not be in the current situation she was in. Her determination is what fuels me today.

My father was a young man that loved fishing and having people around him all the time. His fight in life was a little different than my mom's, he was more family driven than ambition-driven, or should I say again that he loved to have people around him.

My life seemed perfect to me at that time but in retrospect, there was a lot missing. I thought I had everything and never thought I needed anything more. My parents were growing up and taking care of a young child, so you can imagine that this was difficult for them also.

They were teenagers taking care of a baby. What did that mean? We all grew up together.

Young Parents, con't

There were many times when they wanted to go out on a date and couldn't because of me, but guess who had the opportunity to go to certain venues, ME!

I vividly remember going to a movie with them that terrified me. The name of the movie was "Blackula". I'm not sure why I was taken to this movie, I never really asked but it terrified me so much. I started seeing visions of this fat lady blocking the doorway to my room. I couldn't get passed her to tell my parents what I saw. I think it was that character in the movie named Mamawaldi. LOL! What kind of name is that?

I laugh now but at 4 years old I was traumatized. I think it spawned my love for movies today. I'm telling this story today because I admire that my parents didn't just leave me somewhere or leave me alone in the house, so they could just have a night out on the town together.

Dad was extremely social, so it wasn't strange to see a party or card game happening at our house. The great old school music tunes and dancing happened frequently. Our house seemed as though it was the hangout place on our block. I stayed in my room watching TV but often heard the different genres of music, which now has become a love for me.

For my parents to have some time together, I was able to go outside and play in front of the house with my friends. We lived on a popular but busy street, traffic was constant, and the sidewalks were narrow. We had to figure out how to play our games without getting hit by cars.

My friends and I were playing with a ball and the ball ran into the street, I ran across the street to retrieve it and a truck came speeding down the street, I guess to film a story. The truck struck me and broke my leg. This was the beginning of too much freedom.

Young Parents, con't

My parents and I went to court and God blessed me. He was with me even then. I had no flaws just a broken leg and a nice payout for my injury. This was too much on such young parents and a child to go through but this "Bump Had a Purpose" also in our lives.

"Young parents hold tight to your children even though you're trying to make it also, it won't be easy, but it will spawn a great child if your intentions are not about you."

Let me tell you a little about my parents. My Mom and Dad came from different backgrounds, but both had the same love for me. I never felt as though we didn't have enough, I always thought we were rich because I lacked nothing. I was taken care of the whole time, but I did have a lot of freedom because they had to work and provide for me.

I must say that freedom cost and did get my curiosity up. I got into things that caused me to get on punishment quite a bit. As I grew up, the more freedom the more problems, but because I had that survival nature like my parents, I made it through them all. Now as I'm older, I recognized God had His hand on me the whole time.

With the strength of going through some things, it was easier to tell my father that I was in trouble than to tell my mother.

You're probably saying, "What, I could never tell my Dad?" Well I did, because I didn't want to disappoint my mother. Mom worked so hard to give me a great life and I cared more about what she thought of my actions than my father. My Dad was my buddy, so it was easier to say to him, that I messed up.

I bet your wondering; what kind of relationship was that? Well, we all grew up together and I saw my mom fight hard to get out the situations she was in and how far she came to give me the greatest life I could ever have.

Young Parents, con't

My Dad's life was a little better, so he didn't have to fight as much as my Mom did, I believe he was a little more lenient with me. Was I an obedient child? I was when they were looking, but the enemy was lurking to change my mind when in the dark.

My parents divorced when I was 13 years old and we moved away, this didn't stop the relationship I had with my Dad or Mom. We continued to interact together despite the changes.

Even though my Dad was not faithful to my Mom, I still loved him to the moon and back, he could do no wrong in my eyes. However, I was very protective of my Mom. She was my provider and even though I was going through some things I couldn't tell her what was happening to me, I was afraid of stopping her mission, which was to give us a better life.

Did you have this dilemma with your parents? What about with your children? Do your children have this dilemma with you?

Now that my parents are apart, my Mom is working, and my Dad doesn't live with us any longer, what does that mean for me? More FREEDOM! There was no one there to watch me, or so I thought, God was watching and was with me all the time all.

"FREEDOM CAN MAKE YOU, OR HURT YOU DEPENDING ON HOW YOU EMBRACE IT!"

Here are some things I remember that I was comfortable to tell my parents. (an extremely short), I'm just painting a picture here, so don't get discouraged:

Mom	Dad
I'm Pregnant (once)	I'm Pregnant (two times).
	Dad I need an abortion!
	Let's go drinking!
	Can my boyfriend stay over?

26

Young Parents, con't

This is probably strange to many people, but my Dad was very lenient with me, he was more like my buddy. I'll never know why he was that way with me, he's no longer with us today, so I can't really ask that question. But he allowed me to learn by example and consequence.

I don't want you to think that he was a bad person, but he was just easy going with his baby girl. Was he preparing me to be the woman I am today? I would say yes, but I must say that I believe I was given the option to have both sides of the coin when it comes to great parents.

Each parent brought something different to my life. I had two different perspectives that I can offer the world. I know God placed us all together for a reason.

For this reason, my Mother who is the greatest woman and mother in the world. She's a fighter and a go-getter, she offers me so much wisdom, knowledge, and fight. She's smart and is beautiful inside and out. God allowed her to have me, so I can see the righteousness of God and become the caring woman that I am today.

My Dad was my confidant and my twin but taught me to fight for what I wanted and to stand strong whether it's good or bad. He showed me how to be strong and weak at the same time, which I thought was strange, but has been useful in my adult years.

His complexity intrigued me and gave me the fight I have now. How do you feel about your parents? Are you blaming them for the mistakes, encounters, and issues you got yourself into? Reflect on the good parts of the relationship not the bad. Your parents are here to begin your journey, you're here to finish it!

The enemy wants to steal the good memories we have and cloud our minds, so you can't see that you're the good thing that your parents brought to the world.

Young Parents, con't

A letter to GOD!

Dear God,

I am grateful for the family you gave me, these two young parents had a mission to do and that was to birth a Queen that is strong and courageous, one that will not back down and will stand up and fight but has compassion for people and not just her "four and no more". I am grateful for them. Please take care of my Dad, I know he is truly with you now. I will continue to watch over my Mom who is still guiding me today to be the Woman of God that you have ordained me to be.

Your Faithful Servant and Daughter, Melanie!

MOMENT OF REFLECTION

Young Parents

What's your relationship with your parents? How do you see your parents? I believe that you must take a deep dive into what your life is like. Our parents are the reason that we're alive, they could have decided for us not to be in this world, but they chose you.

Reflect on your parents and see the goodness in both. Understand that if you're reading this and they're on this earth still, they have created you to be a strong person.

If you're a parent now. Ask yourself these questions and think about how these questions pertain to the person you have developed into.

1. Do I speak to my child as though they are destined for success, greatness and godliness?
2. Do I say the following things to my child?
    a. I'm proud of you.
    b. I believe in you.
    c. You can do it!
    d. I'm there for you.
    e. I love you.
    f. You are a King/Queen

If our children hear it from us (the parent) then it becomes difficult for the enemy to come and say the same words (which have a different twist and meaning), they will hear your voice over the crafty nature and the pull of the enemy.

Reflect on these things, this is very important!

Athletics & Education
Chapter 3

ATHLETICS is a great activity for children to partake in. It enhances their physical, emotional, social, educational and other social activities that assist them into adulthood. **High school athletes are more likely than non-athletes to attend college** *and get degrees; team captains, MVPs achieve in school at even higher rates (US Dept. of Education, 2005).* **The benefits extend to the workplace.** *A survey of 400 female corporate executives found 94% played a sport and that 61% say that has contributed to their career success (EY Women Athletes Business Network/espnW, 2014).*

I began my love for sports before I was 10 years old. It started with watching the local guys at our neighborhood park as I mentioned in previous chapters. I'd watch them play basketball and envision myself in the game. The thought of scoring points and the accolades given when you score was intriguing.

I started playing basketball with the local boys and learned all the tricks of the street game. They didn't care that I was a girl, at that time, they just saw me as one of them. Playing in the park everyday made me a stronger person, I even endured pain while playing with the boys, but it taught me how to be tough in the game and now life.

They didn't see me as a girl at that time, so they taught me the toughness of being on the court with them. I sometimes thought they resented me for wanting to play with them, but they allowed me to try it anyway.

It was now time for me to begin my middle school years and I now decided to try out for the school team. The great thing was they had a girls' team for me to play on at our local junior high, which was called South.

Athletics & Education, con't

I immediately began to play, and the coach was amazed that I knew so much about the game at such a young age. This was the beginning of my athletic career. Even though it was great for me to participate in, it caused a lot of rivalry from friends and sometimes even family members. I was good at what I did on the court. I had a hidden talent that took me far.

During this great time for me, my parents were going through a separation which caused me to leave my old school and go the rival school across town. The school was North Junior High and the coaches were familiar with who I was, since we have played against each other for a few years.

My parents split up and we (Mom and I) moved from the Heights to across town with my maternal grandmother (a Preacher). She lived in a three-story house that housed all of us, my two aunts and their 5 children on the top floor, my uncle, his wife and their 4 boys on the second floor, on the first floor was My grandparents, my two uncles and now add in the basement Me and My Mom, plus my aunt and her daughter at that time. We had so much fun playing in the house.

Mom had to work late nights to take care of us and try and change our situation. She was focused on providing for us. Once we moved from the Heights to across town as we called it, I had to change schools because of district rules. I now began my next semester at rival school North Junior High. Once I came to North the coach recognized me because we played against them many times, during our big rival game. I demonstrated my abilities even though she knew my skill level. The coach asked me to demonstrate some moves under the basket, while guarding me under the basket she ended up on the floor.

I didn't realize I was that strong, especially not strong enough to break her leg. After that incident I received an automatic starting spot on the team.

Athletics & Education, con't

Coach thought I was too intense for such a young child, but this intensity is what spawned the rest of my athletic career and my fight in life.

We played a few more games and years against my old rival school, the gym was packed because I had some great friends on South that were awesome players also, this rivalry continued until we entered high school. My athletic career kicked off because basketball made my name great in New York.

Mom got a great job and I had to leave my school and friends. I was scheduled to go to the 9th grade the next year, but the great thing was the new school started at 9th grade in high school. If I stayed in Newburgh, I would still be in junior high in the 9th grade. I was in heaven now, all my friends that played with me in Newburgh were still playing on the junior high team and now I get to play at the varsity level in Poughkeepsie. This was the beginning of the best four years of my life.

Sports fans in Poughkeepsie knew me because I played on summer teams and played against them in junior high. I was on a sports high from all the accolades I received.

It's now the beginning of 9th grade and my first time in high school. Things are different in this school, but I liked it. I had a 6'5' African American female principal, who didn't play around with children, her demeanor terrified us. But she had so much wisdom. I remember to this day every great thing she told me and taught me about being a woman and being successful in life.

I was blessed to have the best coaches in my career, my high school volleyball, softball coach and my basketball coach (who was like a father to me). All of them poured into me and taught me how to conduct myself in every situation and to be a leader and not a follower.

Athletics & Education, con't

I spent countless hours with my coaches and they shaped my life and my toughness. Athletics, however is what really shaped me. I excelled in this school, I was Class President for 4 years, Honored in All Sports for 4 years.

However, basketball is what fueled me and gave me the drive to be a leader. The state championship runs and the comradery with great players by your side allowed me to be the person I am today.

I could have chosen any scholarship for any sport, but I chose to excel in Basketball. Basketball allowed me to be honored in the state of New York having over 2000 career points and 1000 rebounds.

New York has games similar to the Olympics in the state called the Empire State Games. The committee surveys all the students in the state and pick only a few to represent in the games. I was fortunate enough to play two years in a row with a co-player of mine to represent New York State. These games housed the best of the best

There were many players from New York that were taken to the NBA to play at that time. I was away in training for the games, for two weeks in Syracuse, NY, there were days I was wiped out. But the fight in these games made me who I am today. I exude strength and confidence in everything I do.

I am a fighter now for the Lord, the same intensity God had given me in sports, I use today in Ministry.

These games were viewed by many college scouts around the country and now I have a choice to receive a scholarship for the school of my choosing. I could've attended anywhere in the country but decided to go to a school in Dobbs Ferry, NY (outside of Bronx, NY) a Division 2 NCAA school, where my coach from the Empire State Games began my collegiate career.

Athletics & Education, con't

I chose this school because I wanted to be near my parents in hope that they would come and watch me play. But they had the opportunity to see all my games.

I've always been one to understand things practically. I believe I'm a systematic thinker, not really scattered and have always wanted to lead. I wasn't a follower. I believe I got those qualities from my Mom. I excelled in my class; my teachers adored me and often saw the leader in me. I have an uncanny way of assisting people. My teachers and then later professors saw my potential also. Things just fell in my lap. This is how I knew that God had a greater plan for my life.

I was class president for 4 years and never had a running mate. The students all said, *"you won't win if you go up against her"*. I didn't have a lot of friends just a small crew and an entourage. Which I didn't want either? This could cause problems. Which it did in college?

My college years where full of workouts, dorm rooms and too much freedom. For some reason they kept all the Athletes in a co-ed dorm which I thought was cool, at that time. As I got older, it became a real problem.

We played Tag in the middle of the night and the boys were in the room next to mine. When we took a shower after a workout, beware of cold buckets of water being poured on you in the shower. There was just too much going on in the dormitory and way too much freedom.

The one thing I enjoyed about college was the accolades I received because I was a basketball player. However, too much fame can take you into dark places. You begin to feel as though your famous and soon your head begins to swell. I was popular on the yard and that means you're seen by others and they want to be around you.

Athletics & Education, con't

I was approached by men (or boys) and women (curious girls), by drugs and sheer danger and those things soon took its toll on me. There were nights when I was given things just so people can spend some time with me. This opened me up to a dark world that I shouldn't have entered. A realm that I was not prepared to be in.

I had encounters with those that wanted my time. This all took a toll on me and my education soon ceased with a torn ligament in my knee. This caused my fame to go away and my grades also.

I had to reevaluate this, so I left and went to Atlanta, GA still searching for my purpose.

"You don't look out there for God, something in the sky, you look in you." Alan Watts

"Even in disaster try and be the best you, you can be." Know that this "bump too had a purpose".

I was made for this journey and have survived it also.

MOMENT OF REFLECTION

Athletics & Education

How do we get our children to focus? How can we alert them of the dangers that can scare them so much they don't want to try it? God made you and your offspring great, but we all seek something contrary to what God's plan is. Why?

I believe we need to tell our story to them, so they can see the triumph in you. Look to God and Live. I was reading an article, and this stuck out at me. The writer mentioned, *"We know that some of the world's most painful suffering is done in silence, in the sorrow of a lonely life."* I believe we all feel lonely at times, but don't forget God is walking with you daily. You're never alone with God.

1. Are you searching for something to fulfill your life?
2. Do you know the only fulfillment you need is to understand that God is with you?
3. Evaluate the heart of people and you'll see if they have good intentions.
4. Be the best person you can be, and your actions will determine your fate.

Reflect on this statement: *"What does God want from me?"*

_____

_____

_____

_____

_____

_____

_____

_____

My Strength Was Their Problem
(the Violators)
Chapter 5

Strength is a bad word to some people, especially for those that are insecure with themselves. It can make you or break you. I always believed when I was younger that I was a pillar of strength until the series of things in my life told me I might be strong in mind but weak in stature.

I always had a great connection with boy's/men, but they were always intimidated by me, so they felt they had to show me I wasn't strong and who was in charge. I remember playing on a recreation basketball team with mostly boys and only two girls. The boys would tease me and since I began to develop faster than most girls. This is where they noticed that I was a girl and not a player of theirs. They began to see the differences and it was drastic.

Game days were great until the boys started experiencing feelings for their teammates. After games our coach allowed us to go in and change before the boys changed, but some of the boys decided they were coming into the shower also. This was the second violation in my young life and then I realized I wasn't a regular team member any longer.

I ran home and told my uncles about what happened, and they soon ran to the recreation center to defend me. This was the first of those incidents where they (my violators) felt they had strength and power over me.

I was a little puzzled because I didn't understand fully why they felt that way. Who could I talk to about this? I survived it and God was indeed with me even during this time. Amen!

My Strength Was Their Problem (the Violators), con't

Strength is something that is underrated and needs to be defined;

"the definition of strength is a good or beneficial quality or attribute of a person or thing (Google Dictionary)."

This trend continued throughout my life, I've always been a confident and caring person, but it seemed my confidence frightened my violators.

In my dating years I seemed to attract boyfriends that always wanted to show their strength and needed to show me that I was weaker than them. Why was I such a threat to them? Did you ever feel like that? I really wasn't sure where that came from. Was it me or was it them? I exuded confidence in most things I did. I used to believe I got this confidence from my dad, but I realize God made me confident and this was a purposeful attribute for me.

I was always looking for love in the wrong places because this seemed to be what I was attracted to. What was I doing wrong? Was I in a whirlwind? Why am I attracted the same kind of person? Why was I attracted to someone that was insecure with themselves and that wanted to dominate others?

I've had some strange experiences in my life, some I don't truly understand and some I believe were intentional. One I vividly recall is an old boyfriend of mine who I thought was the most gorgeous man in the world. Boy was I wrong, his outside looked good but the heart was bad.

He treated me so nice in the beginning of our relationship until he moved me away from my family. This is when we moved to Atlanta, Georgia and the terror began.

My Strength Was Their Problem (the Violators), con't

Have you ever been verbally, mentally and physically abused? I was so terrified of coming home late for fear of the abuse intensifying. I thought, why am I being treated this way? Even though I was afraid, I was still afraid to express myself about the situation.

I was battered daily, which took a toll on me. The strange thing is God must have been with me, because I existed in two spaces. The outside world didn't know I was hurting or being abused at all. I camouflaged it so well that I convinced myself to exist in two worlds and thought nothing was wrong.

When we went on outings, I would get dressed up to attend the events, but he would tell me how ugly and fat I was. I couldn't understand what he meant because at that time I had a basketball body and I was young (so I was looking fine). I thought I was cute (Lol) but he insisted and told me I was fat, ugly and never would be able to walk with him. This is just the short of the abuse I took from him.

No matter how strong you think you are, the enemy will play with your mind to get you to do the inevitable, to kill yourself and to remove yourself from the abuse. He even tries to make you feel not worthy to be on this earth. Well that was the state I was in. I decided to end it and then the phone rang. We received a call from a mutual friend of ours that was now a Minister in the Faith and he began to minister to me at that time. I was extremely shocked by his transformation because I knew him when he was in the world.

I quickly told him that He (my abuser) wasn't at home and he said to me, *"leave you will make it, you are worth it to God"*. The weird thing is, I never told him what was happening, even when he visited us. Remember, I was the master of camouflage.

My Strength Was Their Problem (the Violators), con't

I took his advice and then packed a small bag and got on the bus headed to Austin, Texas where my grandmother lived. This was 1988 (my first flee to Texas).

My grandmother embraced me and then proceeded to help me get back on my feet. But she was a person that felt no matter what happens to you should make it right if it's a good person. But to me he wasn't good and wasn't good for me. I thought if I go back and work things out with this evil person would it be better? He called my grandmother's house and she told him where I was. He tried to come to get me. I left to go to New York, and then my running began.

Your violators may look good, but what is God saying to you about this person?

Violators can also come from church environments. Once I got back to New York, I met some wonderful ladies that had a large women's group. I began to go to several gatherings and retreats and then joined a Baptist Church and the ladies kept trying to get me saved and find me a mate. I think they were being a little pushy in this area.

The Bible says, *"He that finds a [true and faithful] wife finds a good thing and obtains favor and approval from the Lord" (Prov. 18:22 AMP)* not *"The women in your group that find you a husband is a good thing." LOL!*

The ladies introduced me to one of the young ministers in the church. We went out on a few dates and spent a little time together, but then it was suggested that we get married. We began counseling, we took all the classes and then they wanted to marry us quickly. I should've seen the signs because this was moving too fast.

40

My Strength Was Their Problem (the Violators), con't

I went to his home one evening to talk to him about us moving so fast, he of course wanted to do more since we were away from the church and we were alone. He was a wolf in sheep clothing, so I advised him that we should wait. Most times we are unaware of *wolves in sheep clothing. Being* unaware of them allows you to fall for anything.

When I refused his advances, he forced me down on the floor and continued to overpower me. I fought hard to keep him off me. I shouldn't have gone to his place anyway. My instincts told me no, but I kept trying to do this my way. We began to tussle over a dispute, and he overpowered me and held me down on the floor.

He began to rip my clothing and I fought him off then I felt something weird in his shirt. It sounded like paper (I heard a crumpling noise). This was weird, strange and all those other words.

I tried to wrestle with him and was able to see what was in his shirt, he had my name and picture written on paper and it was taped to his chest. I had never seen anything that strange before, so I knew I was dealing with something that was demonic.

I was able to wrestle him off me, but then I started looking on the walls and he had pictures on the walls, on the backs of pictures he had my picture and name there, this freaked me out so bad that I got a knife out of the kitchen to defend myself and to keep him off me.

I had never in my life seen something so satanic, I grabbed the phone and called one of the head ministers at church to let them know what was about to happen and where I was. This made me leave the church and try to live a different life away from religion. This was straight up witchcraft.

REMEMBER THIS:

"YOU NEVER KNOW HOW STRONG YOU ARE, UNTIL BEING STRONG IS THE ONLY CHOICE YOU HAVE."

Also

"THE STRUGGLE YOU'RE IN TODAY IS DEVELOPING THE STRENGTH YOU NEED FOR TOMORROW"

I left God, but He was still walking with me.

MOMENT OF REFLECTION

My Strength Was Their Problem (the Violators)

How do you move on after such a tragedy? You do it with the unwavering love of God. I remembered clearly a song that I still listen to today, *"Save Me Now"* by Commissioned. Since the abuse in all situations was so awful, I thought that I deserved it, I thought that I was lower than, and that I didn't deserve to be here any longer. I wanted to take away the pain, not really thinking about my father and mother's pain if I had accomplished it. I was sitting on the floor and playing a cassette tape by Commissioned and the song just ministered to my soul. I listen to that same song today to remind me of my success in coming out.

Sister and even brother if it's happening to you, I'm a living witness that God is always there. He doesn't walk away from us, it's us who leaves Him. He just wants us to surrender and turn back to Him. He wants us to find him and commune with His Glory.

1. Sometimes the strongest women are those who love beyond all faults, cry behind closed doors, and fight battles that nobody knows about. -author: unknown
2. A strong woman knows she has strength enough for the journey, but a woman of strength knows it's in the journey where she will become strong.
3. Evaluate the heart of people and you will see if they have good intentions.

Reflect on this statement: *"I will give thanks and praise to You, for I am fearfully and wonderfully made; Wonderful are Your works, and my soul knows it very well." (Psalm 139:14 AMP)*

43

7 Pregnancies and No Births
Chapter 6

Introduction

This chapter was the hardest of all to write, I often felt even in my older age that I wasn't worthy of bringing life into the world. I felt that God wasn't pleased with me and didn't trust me with children. I thought that I was good enough to impart all the knowledge and fight He gave me into them. Well, this wasn't the case.

When a woman has a baby, they feel as though they're now a real woman. They have conquered the quest, which is motherhood. *"Motherhood is an opportunity for creative spiritual growth and transformation in women"* according to Aurelie M. Athan and Lisa Miller of Spiritual awakening through the Journey of Motherhood. There is a connection created when a woman becomes a mother.

This was me! I had always felt as though I wasn't good enough to bring children into the world. Each time I got pregnant, I either aborted them, because of the circumstances or had miscarriages. Miscarriage after miscarriage, abortions after abortion and pain after pain, I never understood why this was happening to me. I often wondered if I was a misfit or I was damned by God because of my previous antics in life.

I remember clearly the voice of my mother as she rushed me to the hospital because the baby was aborting while we were in the car. Her comment was, *"It's just not in the stars for you."* My question was, *"why not me"?* I think I would've been a good mother for my children. But was I ready for all that?

Freedom is lost, time is lost, I still hadn't grown up myself. It really had nothing to do with me the person. It wasn't in God's plan for me at that time. I asked myself often, could I be a good mother? Would I have been neglectful?

7 Pregnancies and No Births, con't

I know now that if I had children of my own, I would've never met my King, my friend and my love. I also wouldn't have been able to affect all the children I mentor and those I coached for almost 20 years. I wouldn't be able to spend time mentoring today.

I would've been one of those women that could only give my time and attention to my own children, now I'm Aunt Mel to many children around the world.

What I realized in my search for God's love was that His plan was much bigger than my four and no more. I was brought into this world to assist in fulfilling the call for many children not just my own and I accept the charge.

I finally realized that even though God didn't fulfill the desire I had to have my own children, He fulfilled so much more than that.

He's given me great gifts and allowed me to be open to share my gift of being one of the greatest servants He has ever had. There are many children in my life today that I minister to and show them a better way

That pit in my stomach still sat there at times, I was still feeling that I wasn't good enough, but as I searched for other women that where barren but still affected the lives of many, I realized I wasn't alone in this area. These women were childless also but affected many people in the world.

They have inspired me also. I too can make a difference in other's lives. Look at the role models we can be inspired by:

- **Abrahams Wife Sarai** (God changed her barren nature)
- **Rebekah** (She was barren for 20 years but her and Isaac's prayer and trust in God gave them twins 20 years later)
- **Samson's mother**, (she birthed a son with prodigious strength).

7 Pregnancies and No Births, con't

These are just a few in the bible. If it's possible for them then it's possible for me. Let's look at more women that were barren that pioneered before my time.

- **Harriet Tubman** – Barren but saved many slaves and changed the world. She also in her older age was able to adopt a child.
- **Rosa Parks** – The pioneer that refused to get up after a hard day at work and worked tirelessly on changing laws for African Americans. She changed the culture.

I'm in no way comparing myself to these great women, but their barrenness allowed me to see that there is good that comes with being in this condition and I'm grateful for it.

This should encourage you:

Dear Childless Mother,

I hold you up on a pedestal of greatness, of love, of merciful strength. And if I would define motherhood the very depths of what it is. I would describe you. You are more of a mother than I could ever be. Themomcafe.com

MOMENT OF REFLECTION

7 Pregnancies and No Births

I'm so grateful that I saw the light. God knew that there would be limitations on my life if He allowed me to have children. Several things would have happened:

1. I wouldn't have made a difference in many lives (all the children and people that I encountered thus far)
2. I wouldn't have met my King if I had multiple children hanging on my hip, because God told him what to look for.
3. I wouldn't have time to affect the world in bringing the Kingdom of Heaven here on earth which will heal many children in the world.

Are you still wondering, *why is life like this for me*? *Why don't I have what they have? Why am I barren*? If you're thinking like this, then turn your thoughts towards Him.

Isaiah 55:8-9 AMP says, *"For my thoughts are not your thoughts, nor are your ways My ways, declares the Lord. For the heavens are higher than the earth, so are My ways higher than your ways and My thoughts higher than your thoughts".*

This means He knows what your path is, what you're capable of and what He has for you to do in the earth. Embrace that! Know that God is the author and finisher of your fate. **Hebrews 12:2 (NKJV, partial).**

Failed Relationships
Chapter 7

Introduction

Love is one of the most profound emotions known to human beings. There are many kinds of love, but most people seek its expression in a romantic relationship with a compatible partner. For some, a heartfelt relationship is the most meaningful element of life, providing a source of deep fulfillment in self. Having a healthy, loving relationship is not innate. You must work at having a good relationship and remember it takes two to make it work.

Even though I was the life of many parties and extremely popular, that too cost me because you attract all types of people, and I mean ALL types. Everyone wants your time and want to bring you into their world. I believe that popularity cost me at times, because there were people the enemy put in my path to derail my calling.

I won't recap every relationship I've ever had, that would make this chapter long, but I can tell you this, *"all that glitters ain't gold"*. I never really dated anyone my age, because of my maturity level, plus I was always attracted to people that were older than me. I just thought I would fit better with them. I was the oldest grandchild and an exuded strength so I felt I could handle anything. I was also a person that everyone wanted to get advice from.

With control comes fluff and intrigue, once the intrigue is gone, you're now just a regular person, you're seen as too young to know anything. They now had requirements for me and wanted me to be submissive to them and the situation. They even begin to take rule over me.

Failed Relationships, con't

Being mature doesn't make you, but it will break you, especially if you're willing to walk into a level of maturity your mind can't handle.

I will just list out what I encountered, not to go into too much detail because it will take up more than a chapter to tell you about it (laugh).

- High School Dream Boat (or so I thought)
- College relationships (too many to name)
- Popularity Dates (just wanted my time and me)
- The man of my dreams (or so I thought)
- Random Tries
- My disingenuous love (confusion)

I've had my share of silliness in relationships, failed love or no love from others. Most people just wanted the fame of being with or around me, not sure why though. The man of my dreams was an abuser and full of himself. The random tries were me trying to fill a void in my life, but I should've turned to God.

What was I really thinking? I thought they could bring me happiness by entertaining all this craziness. Well, you see that didn't happen.

With all the failures and me trying to find and want someone to love me for me, I failed when it came to men, so I decided to change sides.

After all the trauma of relationship with men, I met a very nice lady that soon became my plus 1. I thought I found an awesome person and she had two darling children, so that completed my family. Have you ever heard the term, confused? Confused means, *unable think clearly, bewildered* (Google dictionary). I entered an area that wasn't for me and tried to survive in it.

Failed Relationships, con't

This is how I knew I wasn't close to God. I began to change the design that God had created for man and for me, I fell in love. I had a family (but not a traditional one), I even planned a wedding. Again, what was I thinking? Where was I in my walk with God? I left him. He didn't leave me. The Bible says this about confusion:

> " For God is not the author of confusion but of peace..." I Corinthians 14:33 (NKJV) partial

Was I at peace? I thought I was, I seemed happy, but there were times when I didn't really understand what I had gotten into. This was different from the other encounters in my life, I now had a full fledge family.

Was I walking with God in this situation? God made us male and female and now I'm walking contrary to what God's plan and design was for humanity and for me.

I had a sense of false happiness in this relationship. I was so upset with the treatment I experienced with men that I accepted anyone's love. This is the start of a very trying time in your mind and your self-esteem.

MOMENT OF REFLECTION

Failed Relationships

Do you feel as though all your relationships were bad and you're going in the wrong direction? Well, that could be true, listen to that still small voice that's talking to you. If you feel as though it's wrong, then it's probably wrong. That check in your spirit is the consciousness of God. The tugging (thoughts or that still small voice) is God pursuing you. God Bless!

Reevaluate the relationships you had in the past and in the present and write down how you want your future relationships to be. Define it! It will help you when you encounter it.

_____

_____

_____

_____

_____

_____

_____

Do you have a consciousness towards God? Use the woman at the well as an example.

Living A Contrary Lifestyle
(The Revelation)
Chapter 8

Introduction

How do you know you're not supposed to be in this realm if you don't listen to that still small voice in your head?

I entered a world that I didn't belong in, but I thought I was put there for a reason. I needed help deciphering the new world I was in, so my social circle changed. I went deeper and deeper into this world with no help or guidance. I told my parents about my new situation and that I met a woman, remember the chapter of my parents, I mentioned that one was more lenient than the other when it came to me. I told my mother about my new love. She wasn't that happy about it and didn't really discourage me at that time. I told dad also who was ok with whatever I did.

Here is where it got strange, my partner asked me to marry her. We began setting the plans, we got matching tattoos. My life was now spiraling out of control. I had a full fledge family to take care of and wasn't sure how this all happened so fast. The inevitable came, the wedding day, I got married in a church but not to a man, my mom wasn't in attendance, my dad came but again he was more lenient with me.

Let's fast forward some years. Time elapsed and a full fledge family was there. One day in the home, a bullet pierced the house and nearly killed one of the children, so we moved, this was strike one! The next house we moved to, there was gun fire outside the house, so we moved again, strike two!

This last time I realized I never lived like this before, why is tragedy following me? Could it be that I was following tragedy?

Living a contrary lifestyle, con't

Time and years have passed and on my drive home from work, a voice said to me so clear that I thought someone was in my car, it said, *"this was not what I asked you to do"*. *This* voice was clear as daylight, I thought I was having a moment, but the voice spoke again, and said, *"this was not what I asked of you"*. This prompted me to pull over my car and look in the back seat, but it was empty, this really puzzled me. Confused and bewildered I sat in my car pondering on my next move.

I thought I was going crazy, the voice was clear, and I'd been struggling with where I was in my life. I know that I was upset with past relationships. I lost a great man in my life, but his situation was not conducive to us being together either.

I needed help. The final voice I heard is that I needed to tell my then "spouse" to move out with her children. I told her this was not the life for me. **John 14:26 NKJV** *"But the helper, the Holy Spirit, whom the father will send in My name, He will teach you all things and bring to your remembrance all that I have said to you."*

I knew the calling on my life but didn't want that responsibility at that time. I knew what God said to me, but I didn't want to accept it at that time. I was a different person and people liked being around me (but that means all people). I had to be careful about who and how I encountered a person. I still have friends that are in this life, but that life was not for me.

I did what the Lord told me, I ended this disingenuous lifestyle and began to seek the Lord more. I really needed His guidance. It was a lonely walk because I had to be with God Himself, I needed to be refocused on what I was made for.

Year's passed and finally God sent my King to me, we began to walk with the Lord, but something happened, my ex contacted me and wanted me to visit her and I did. She advised me she too also met an awesome man.

Living a contrary lifestyle, con't

Praise God! She was extremely happy, she also told me she was pregnant and wanted me to be the God Mother. She mentioned that they were getting married and I was extremely happy for her and accepted the charge. At this time, I was married also to my King for a couple of years.

A year passed by and the wedding was coming up, she was so happy and elated, but anxious also, my step-daughter and I assisted her at the wedding and noticed her feet were very swollen. I just thought it was because of all the excitement of the wedding and a little of her high blood pressure.

This wedding day was so exciting for her, she was now ready to walk the aisle. The minister asked her if she wanted to accept Christ and she accepted Christ as her savior (the angels were singing) and then they went off in the sunset for their honeymoon. This was a glorious day.

The next day I received a call from her telling me, "Thank you" for all that we did for her and being a great example to her. She was very happy, something I'd never heard in her before. The following day tragedy happened.

I received a call from her oldest son. He alerted me his mom was in the hospital. I told him I just spoke to her the night before and she told me that this was the best day of her life. What could've happened in such a small timeframe? He told me that she had an aneurism burst while on the honeymoon.

Was it the excitement? We'll never know because she never came home.

I said all this to say this, her new husband today is a Great Man of God. Her son is a Music Minister and has a lovely family. Had I stayed in the situation with her, would I have derailed the plan that God had for them?

Living a contrary lifestyle, con't

This is how I feel about what transpired. We didn't go to church when we were together, so the example wasn't there. It also pushed me to seek Him more and to understand the strength of being Man and Woman in a relationship.

Today, I have the greatest man in the world as a husband. I believe that I am truly his rib. My failed relationships allowed me to be the greatest woman I can be for my family, friends and those I encounter. God's plan for me was much bigger than anything I've ever thought of. What plan does God have for you?

MOMENT OF REFLECTION

Living a contrary lifestyle.

Do you feel like a misfit sometimes and think because you're different that you have the right to walk anywhere you want to go in life? If one group doesn't like you try something different. Well different isn't always a good thing, God created us all in a unique fashion. We are created for a reason. It's by His design, you're unique and wonderful. Now embrace it.

If you're in this lifestyle, do you hear the tugging?

Write down the great things that make you one of the greatest creations that God has made to walk this earth. Remember the anointing destroys the yolk.

_____

_____

_____

_____

_____

_____

_____

_____

_____

It takes a special person to say great things about themselves.

Running from Love
Chapter 9

Introduction

LOVE, how do we define love when you really don't know what it is? The textbook term for Love is this…"*an intense feeling of deep affection*". What does God say about love? In **Galatians 5:23-23 (ESV)** says, *"But the fruit of the Spirit is love, joy, peace, patience, kindness, goodness, faithfulness, gentleness, self-control, against such things there is no law."* Love is something everyone wants to experience but rarely know how to give it.

In my time running away from true love, I learned the true definition of it. I was always looking for people to validate who I am. I encountered people that didn't want to show it. These are the things you saw in the chapters before. When you find love, it does something to your heart, it makes you feel as though you're an intentional being.

I remember meeting my husband in 1992, I never met a man that was so intense (but in a good way) and confident, those that I encountered in my past were more about themselves than more about me. The love of my life wasn't far away from me, but his intensity scared me.

I was so used to the uncaring intensity that I felt for many years that I couldn't get past the mask of my hurt. I didn't know what this kind of love was or how to react to it. My past situations were volatile, self-centered and uncaring interactions.

I remembered the day I met him, he would bring me flowers and give me these heartfelt cards. He would ride by the bus stop to see if I was there and offer me a ride. He would just be everywhere I was.

Running from Love, con't

This type of intensity scared me, remember I had a controlling person in previous chapters that controlled my every move, so this seemed similar and I didn't want to go into that realm again.

Ladies, sometimes God is right before your eyes, but we can't get past the pain in our hearts to see the Glory of God. I remember praying years before, *"God please send me someone I can love."* *Selah (in Hebrew, this term is interpreted as a pause to breathe and reflect on the important words)*

We started to date but it wasn't time for us to be together, so we had to part ways for some years to fix the issues in each of our lives. Timing was everything with this relationship. What do I mean? I wasn't ready to be a wife and he certainly didn't want me in the state I was in, and I didn't want him the way he was.

There had to be some God moves in this, if we were meant to be, then God would allow it to happen. Why did I run from him? Was it hurt from others? Was it my past? Was it my present lifestyle? Why run?

The reason I ran was this, I wasn't whole, and why should I give someone something that is not whole. I wasn't ready to commit, I wasn't ready to change and mesh, I wanted things to be done my way and didn't want any input from anyone.

This is very important, the definition of WHOLE is (Google definition): all; the entire, completed, full unabridged, in an unbroken or undamaged state, in one piece. It's a thing that is complete in itself; it's all of something.

Running from Love, con't

The Bible states in 1 Thessalonians 5:23 (AMP)

23 Now may the God of peace Himself sanctify you through and through [that is, separate you from profane and vulgar things, make you pure and whole and undamaged - consecrated to Him - set apart for His purpose]; and may your spirit and soul and body be kept complete and [be found] blameless at the coming of our Lord Jesus Christ.

This is what being whole is, I wasn't there yet.

Genesis 2:24 "Therefore a man shall leave his father and his mother and hold fast to his wife, and they shall become one flesh. I wasn't ready for this either."

Are you?

What does hold fast mean? To hold fast means to be tightly secured or anchored to something. Are you anchored to the Lord? I often asked myself that question but being a woman who does stand out, let me give you some more examples. Let's try Hezekiah which was trusting God, he held fast to God, like we should also. He also obeyed His instructions. What does that really mean in society today? Look at all the examples in this world we live in now.

Trusting is something people have a hard time doing, especially if they are in a broken state.

Trusting God seems to be difficult to us, but to Him who created us, it's simple. God asked for some big things from those who followed Him. Abraham was asked to sacrifice his son Isaac, David defeated a giant with a handful of rocks, Peter walked on water, Paul was shipwrecked but survived it, and God's own Son, Jesus hung on a cross to save the world.

59

Running from Love, con't

If we are believers and truly believe that He can lead us, then why not trust Him to do it? His love and grace will be enough. It might seem difficult; It might even be painful in the process, but it'll also be worth it. You may stumble in the process, but your *"bumps have a purpose"* in your life.

This means the storms of life may create rage, but you don't wander from His side when it happens. Know that your soul is anchored in the Lord.

I never understood what God was putting together with my now husband. He was the balance I needed in life. Where I'm weak, he's strong, where I'm strong, he's weak. I feel as though I'm his rib, we're the perfect balance for each other.

We were made for each other but there were trials we had to walk through to get in this place of peace. He is the man I was looking for all my life, someone that was not afraid of the strength God has given me.

He is a teacher and doesn't judge me concerning my past or my present. He is God's Man, and I am honored to be his wife and friend.

I wasn't whole with the others I encountered in life because I did things backwards, I sought people first instead of seeking God first!

"Dear God,

Thank you for preparing this great king, your son and servant. This is the man you ordained to be in my life. He is your man servant and I am your woman servant. Together we will do the work you have planned for us to accomplish."

Dr. Mel

MOMENT OF REFLECTION

Running from Love

Do you feel like you're meeting the wrong mate, or you just don't fit in the relationship you're in. Who picked who? Did you like how they dressed, or how they walked or what they had?

Did you pray about it? Did you get an answer from God? Did you jump the gun for whatever your reason was?

Write down the characteristics that the Bible says about a man/woman in your life? Do they display the things that God has set in your heart? Remember, the enemy comes to steal, kill and destroy and doesn't want us to be with the person God sent us, this is because *YOU WILL NEVER BE AT YOUR FULL POTENTIAL IN LIFE, WITH THE WRONG MATE.* Be honest with yourself in this reflection.

_____

_____

_____

_____

_____

_____

_____

_____

Accepting My Calling
Chapter 10

Introduction

I never saw this coming, until I met my husband. I didn't feel as though I was worthy of being a Minister, teaching the Word or even speaking in front of crowds. Why me? I asked God one day, and He said, "*why not you, daughter*". I had a presence with people and they even liked talking to me and hearing what I have to say. I understood the Law of Magnetism; it says who you are is who you attract. The good thing is that there is also a Law of Connection it states that the heart comes before the head. If you want to inspire someone or win them over, you must connect with them first. I was always that person. God knew I had the qualities of a good leader, I can't make the mistake of expecting people to come to me, I'm that go getter He needs. Leaders must be available, share appreciation, listen and be willing to get to know people.

Now, this did hurt a little because people wanted to be around me all the time in my previous lives. I began to apply that same energy I had then to God, then people will want to hear how He saved me. I'm a survivor after all the tragedies that tried to overtake me. I never stopped thinking about how my situation could be better.

God knew the strength I had, of course He did, He created me. I was built to do this. I never wanted to be called a preacher, minister or anything, but God placed me in platforms that developed who I am and what I am to be in the earth. He made this Dr. Mel package for His use.

Accepting My Calling, con't

God says to the snow, *"Fall on the earth.* Nothing more, just fall! *Do that one thing, Just fall."* He then says to the rain, *"Be a mighty downpour."* What He was saying is, "do the thing *I've created you for, and do it for me".*

You are rain … so rain. You are snow … so snow. You are Dr. Mel, daughter spread the gospel and show them how to be the light in tough situations. Also show them how to overcome obstacles that are placed before them.

I come from a long line of Pastors, Bishops, and Ministers from my great grandmother, to my grandmother, to most of my uncles. I was no stranger to who God was. I was adamant not to follow the footsteps of those before me, rules were strict, rituals were present, and I never saw them explain the gospels that made me want to stay.

Some of the focus, I believe, was too much on not watching TV shows and wearing clothes that covered me up. I truly rebelled with that thought, it made no sense on why that was a requirement and it was 100 degrees in Texas during summer months (LOL). I wasn't going to wear what they suggested and sweat to death, remember I was from New York where they have changing seasons through the year. But God, will do the changing for you. Once you know Him you will begin to walk in the glory he has for you.

I was playing basketball in college and remembered asking my family members to come to a game to support me, their responses were "*church people don't go to games*" and "*they don't go to movies*". I wondered why they viewed the same shows on the TV at home. I was curious where those words were in the bible. It all seemed so ritualistic. This and other rituals turned me away from following God.

Accepting My Calling, con't

I didn't want to display this false notion to people that you have to be a hermit to serve God. I challenged those who brought that spirit to me, and I was of course ostracized afterwards.

Without naming some of the other things I know God wasn't pleased with, I just decided not to pursue after this religious spirit that I was being introduced to.

I spent the next few years learning and searching for who I was to be in God's eyes. I was already different, I spoke my mind, I'm strategic and exuded great confidence in myself (at least that was on the outside), but I still had a hard exterior that God had to work on. I was raw clay that needed to be transformed.

My husband and I had been married for a little while now, but we knew there we needed something more. As we searched from church to church to find this special something, pain did come with it. I grew up Pentecostal, he grew up Baptist, so we tried each to see if we fit in that picture. There was something different that kept tugging at us.

We met many preachers on our journey to seek more from God. We met a preacher in Texas that preached about the Spirit of God. This was very intriguing to us. The message was something I hadn't heard before and it spoke to my confused soul. The message of the Spirit of God was something I was excited about and I knew this was for me. The good thing is my husband thought the same thing.

I soon learned that it's the Spirit of God that helps you transform into the person He needs you to be.

Accepting My Calling, con't

He gives you gifts to operate in your daily life that will help you transform from those that are contrary to the word of God. They are: wisdom, understanding, counsel, fortitude, knowledge, piety, and fear of the Lord.

I soon learned that having the Spirit of God operating your daily life was the way to go. My next question is how do I perfect it? What do I do to show that I'm following God's path for me?

Well, let me tell you, it's very simple it starts with ensuring you have given your life to Him truly and then utilizing the tools given which are the fruits of the spirit, *Galatians 5:22-24 (AMP) states, "But the fruit of the Spirit [the result of His presence within us] is love [unselfish concern for others], joy, [inner] peace, patience [not the ability to wait, but how we act while waiting], kindness, goodness, faithfulness, gentleness, self-control. Against such things there is no law."*

Walking with Him changes your mind (**M**ain **I**ngredient **N**avigating your **D**estiny), soul and your emotions about things. You're at peace with life and at peace about your assignment.

However, it's a daily walk that drives you to be successful. Once I realized who I was and what Jesus did for me on the cross, my life completely changed and transformed me to do the work and serve Him. I have no problem sharing my testimony to bring others to this wonderful relationship I have today.

If you give your life to the Father, the Father gives life back to you and more abundantly. I now can tell all, preach the word and share the goodness of God with others. In 2016, I was licensed as a Minister and on track to continue to do the work of the Lord.

MOMENT OF REFLECTION
Accepting My Calling

Is everything that you put your hands to, not working? Do you feel like you can make a difference, but you're not equipped to get the message across? Do you feel as though you want a change? Does the life you're living feel incomplete?

Is the life you're living moving you in the right direction? If you're feeling this way, try Jesus, but really try him. God is no respecter of persons. He doesn't care what you have been through. God, just wants you to come to Him and confess and move forward. He's waiting on us we aren't waiting on Him.

_____

_____

_____

_____

_____

_____

_____

_____

_____

_____

Try Jesus!

My Kingdom Adventure
Chapter 11

Introduction

In 2008, I met a group ministers and others that loved the Lord during a conference in Florida. What I enjoyed about these people was the way they explained the Spirit of God and had this uncanny love and passion for people.

This was my first encounter (out of all these years) where I saw a display of the true Spirit of God. People who were able to blend and be around people not like them and illuminate the true Spirit of God. They had this undying respect for the Spirit.

I now understood why my bumps were in my path, it was preparing me to be a vessel for those that experienced the things I went through. I love the term "went through" it means I didn't get stuck during the process; I came out. I was able to experience it and come through it to help others.

I truly believe that God caused an ambush for me to get me into things He has for me now. He wanted me to praise my way through my situations and I did that, but was I ready at that time? The thing that tried to kill me, killed itself. This is when I allowed the process to complete itself. I finally gave in to the Spirit of God and allowed it to overtake me. I surrendered!

God designed us to finish the race, even with a few thorns in our side. Let's talk about that thorn, there is pain in Ministry and why shouldn't it be? Grace = Strength.

My Kingdom Adventure, con't

Everything I went through, experienced and still going through has purpose. 2 Corinthians 12:9b (AMP) states *"for [My] power is being perfected [and is completed and shows itself most effectively] in [your] weakness"*. My weakness is still here to be a teachable moment for me and others. I must go through the process to alert people of how strong God is.

Paul says in 2 Corinthians 12:10 (AMP), *"So I am well pleased with weaknesses, with insults, with distresses, with persecutions, and with difficulties, for the sake of Christ; for when I am weak [In human strength), then I am strong [truly able, truly powerful, truly drawing from God's strength]"*.

As I walk in the newness of my calling, I realize that everything I went through was for those that are coming behind me and for some that have gone before me. I'm here to help people. I'm a living example of success. I'm a living example for those that think there is no other way to live. I'm God's daughter doing the work that He set out for me to do.

I was made to bring the Kingdom of Heaven here on earth. We can have His riches now, we can live a pure and prosperous life now, we can be healed from all our afflictions, now. Do you want to?

I know you hear me talking about the Kingdom, so what is the Kingdom and how can you live in it? I'm glad you asked. The Kingdom is (The **Kingdom of God/Heaven** in the Gospel of Matthew) it's one of the key elements of the teachings of Jesus in the New Testament. It states that since Satan seems to control the world, God is looking for people who will help Him take back His dominion and live.

My Kingdom Adventure, con't

I've always been one that truly understood that if I changed the way I thought about things, then good will come of it. There are times I spoke defeat and it happened, but the opposite also exists. If I speak triumph it also happens. I challenged myself to not see the glass half empty but to see it half full. I changed my perspective on life and repelled negativity.

As I walk in the Glory of God daily, I see things far different than I used to. What do I mean by that? I remember the day when someone approached me and accused me of something I didn't do, rage would creep up and then there was one issue after another.

Now my approach is this, they accused Jesus of everything and crucified him, but He still loved. This is the example I want to live by. When I got mad, I got sick, my head hurt, I ostracized myself and others, I didn't realize this action was not of God.

God is love, He is peace and I choose to live in that same vein with Him. I live by the creed, *"walk like Him, think like Him, and share the knowledge with others"* so they can do the same thing. Does it take time? Yes, but it can be done instantly and with prayer and work with the Father. We're to be the light of the world, and I should walk in that in every situation.

If God is shining in me then I will draw ALL men, Galatians 5:22-23 (AMP) says, *"But the fruit of the Spirit [the result of His presence within us] is love [unselfish concern for others], joy, [inner] peace, patience [not the ability to wait, but how we act while waiting], kindness, goodness, faithfulness, [23] gentleness, self-control. Against such things there is no law."*

My Kingdom Adventure, con't

Let's break this down, I really need you to get this, understanding this will give you freedom if you apply this. It clearly says:

1. **Fruit of the Spirit** (the result of His presence within us). Have you given your life to Him fully? We tend to say we know God, but our actions have yet to catch up with what we say.
2. It also says that **Love** (the unselfish concern for others). This means even your enemies, be concerned for all, even those that despitefully use you.
3. **Joy,** [inner] **Peace, Patience** [not the ability to wait, but how we act while waiting],
4. **Kindness, Goodness and Faithfulness**, these are the most essential in solidifying your position in Him, but these don't work unless you have the previous one.
5. **Gentleness and Self-control**. Gentleness is different, it means meekness and *begins* with the Lord's inspiration and is *finished* by His direction and empowerment. It's a *divinely-balanced* virtue.

I was chosen in my mother's womb to accomplish great things in the earth that will help others. He chose me to lead and I accept the charge. I am to heal the land, open blind eyes and empower people to be better just as He did for me.

As I look back over my life, each bump was a setup to the audience that I'll minister to. It's my charge to assist and demonstrate to people how to transform into the leader that God set them out to be. I must be a living example.

Luke 4:18 (AMP) says, *"The Spirit of the Lord is upon Me, because He has anointed me to preach the gospel to the poor, He has sent me to heal the brokenhearted, to proclaim liberty to the captives and recovery of sight to the blind, to set at liberty those who are oppressed; to proclaim the acceptable year of the Lord."*

My Kingdom Adventure, con't

*Being BLIND is really attacking those in the world today, the acronym for BLIND is **B**asically **L**iving **I**n **N**eed **D**aily (acronym from A Word Fitly Spoken by Dr. Charles Kent). This plagues many people today.*

My Bumps Have a Purpose!! Now I'm charged with sharing the Gospel and helping humanity. Are you willing to assist me?

God Bless!
Dr. Mel

My Bumps!!

But GOD got me through them ALL!

I came through and you can too! Look to GOD!

This illustration and reading this book should

show you how strong you really are?

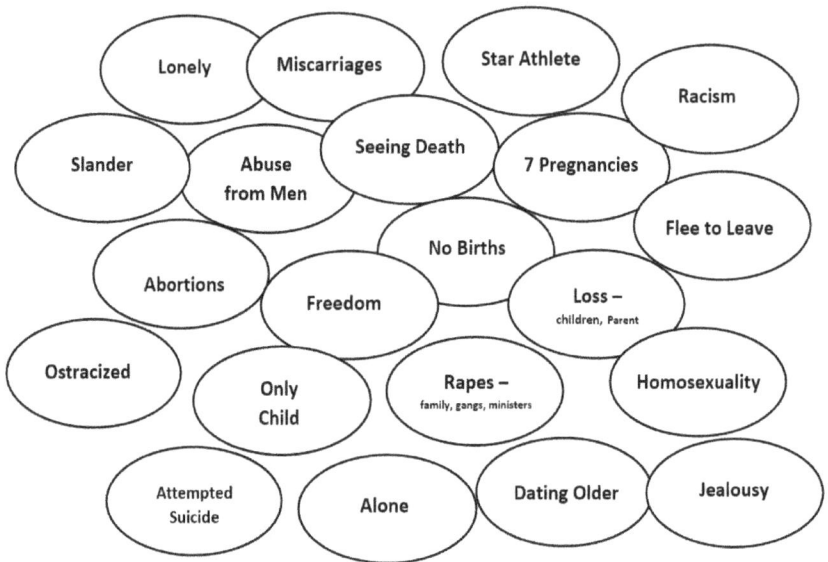

The next pages will help you overcome the things that are plaguing and stopping you from being all that you can be. It will allow you to evaluate, rejuvenate and orchestrate the rest of your life. It can all start here, there is no need to wait, God is calling you now!

My
Declaration
to God!

Write Your Declaration to God
Directions: Tell God what your situation. Ask Him how to get rid of hurt and things you want to be delivered from.

_____
_____
_____
_____
_____
_____
_____
_____
_____
_____
_____
_____
_____
_____
_____
_____
_____
_____
_____
_____
_____
_____
_____
_____
_____
_____
_____
_____
_____
_____
_____
_____

My Spiritual Tool Kit

Tools for your Soul!

LIFE APPLICATION

Now that you made your declaration to God, use these tools in your daily walk to solidify your calling and listen to the things that God wants you to do.

I _____decree and declare:

1. My actions, declarations, decisions and thoughts all **DISPLAY the qualities** of Jesus Christ **AT ALL TIMES**.
2. I'm a good steward of **ALL the things and people GOD has given me** and placed around me.
3. As a Man/Woman of God, I'm a **GODLY partner, wife or husband and a helpmate.** That I compliment and balance them where they are weak and show GODLY strength to my family. **I also DISPLAY HIS qualities so there is no confusion.**
4. **I'm a GODLY Minister of HIS WORD and I display the spirit of LOVE, KINDNESS, and MERCY to ALL, regardless of how I'm treated.**
5. **I WILL BE FAITHFUL** to my ministry and the works that are put before me.
6. **I WILL not misuse the blessings given to me and will use them for GODs Glory.**
7. **I WILL GIVE and be MERCIFUL**, so that I may live the abundant life that HE is giving me.

This is my reasonable sacrifice to Jesus Christ my Lord and Savior.

10 GREAT Bible Verses to Read When You Need DIVINE HELP

Refer to these scriptures when you are dealing with physical and emotional pain. Here are some great bible verses to read when you need healing.

Scripture	Verse
Jeremiah 17:14	"O Lord, if you heal me, I will be truly healed; if you save me, I will be truly saved. My praises are for you alone!"
Proverbs 4:20-22	My son, pay attention to what I say; turn your ear to my words. Do not let them out of your sight, keep them within your heart; for they are life to those who find them and health to one's whole body."
Psalm 34:19	"Many are the afflictions of the righteous, but the Lord delivers him out of them all."
Psalm 147:2	"He heals the brokenhearted and bandages their wounds."
Exodus 15:26	"For I am the Lord who heals you."
Jeremiah 30.17	"I will give you back your health and heal your wounds."
James 5:16	"Therefore, confess your sins to each other and pray for each other so that you may be healed. The prayer of a righteous person is powerful and effective."
2 Chronicles 7:14	"If my people, who are called by my name, will humble themselves and pray and seek my face and turn from their wicked ways, then I will hear from heaven, and I will forgive their sin and will heal their land."

The **WORD OF GOD** in **your mouth** is **stronger than anything** that's ever been said to you.

your **Rx** *Hope Prevails*

What God Says About You
20 Scriptures That Define Your Worth

1. **You are beautiful.** (Psalm 45:11)
2. **You are lovely.** (Daniel 12:3)
3. **You are loved.** (Jeremiah 31:3)
4. **You are chosen.** (John 15:16)
5. **You are special.** (Ephesians 2:10)
6. **You are created in His image.** (Genesis 1:27)
7. **You are cared for.** (Ephesians 3:17-19)
8. **You are strong.** (Psalm 68:35).
9. **You are precious.** (1 Corinthians 6:20)
10. **You are protected.** (Psalm 121:3)
11. **You are unique.** (Psalm 139:13)
12. **You are important.** (1 Peter 2:9)
13. **You are forgiven.** (Psalm 103:12)
14. **You were created for a purpose.** (Jeremiah 29:11)
15. **You are empowered.** (Philippians 4:13)
16. **You are a new creation.** (2 Corin. 5:17)
17. **You are accepted.** (Ephesians 1:6)
18. **You are the apple of His eye.** (Zech. 2:8)
19. **You are family.** (Ephesians 2:19)
20. **You are His.** (Isaiah 43:1)

BIBLE EMERGENCY NUMBERS

A Full List Can Be Found in Google, these assisted me in my transformation.

WHEN ...	CALL IN Number
In Sorrow	Call John 14
Men fail you	Call Psalm 27
You have sinned	Call Psalm 51
You worry	Call Matthew 6:19-24
You are in danger	Call Psalm 91
God seems far away	Call Psalm 139
Your faith needs stirring	Call Hebrews 11
You are lonely and Fearful	Call Psalm 23
You grow bitter and critical	Call I Corinthians 13
You feel down and out	Call Romans 8:31
You want peace and rest	Call Matthew 11:25-30
The world seems bigger than God	Call Psalm 90
You want Christian assurance	Call Romans 8:1-30
You leave home for labor or travel	Call Psalm 121
Your prayers grow narrow or selfish	Call Psalm 67
You want courage for a task	Call Joshua
You think of investments and returns	Call Mark 10
You are depressed	Call Psalm 27
Your pocketbook is empty	Call Psalm 37
Your losing confidence in People	Call I Corinthians 13
People seem unkind	Call John 15
You are discouraged about your work	Call Psalm 126
Self-Pride/Greatness takes hold	Call Psalm 19
You want to be fruitful	Call John 15
You need understanding of Christianity	Call II Corinthians 5:15-19
You have a great invention/opportunity	Call Isaiah 55
You want to know Paul's secret to happiness	Call Colossians 3:12-17

ALTERNATE NUMBERS:

For dealing with Fear	Call Psalm 34:7
For Security	Call Psalm 121:3
For assurance	Call Mark 8:35
For reassurance	Call Psalm 145:18

Please note: Emergency Numbers may be dialed direct. No Operator assistance is necessary. All lines to Heaven are pen 24 hours a day! Feed your faith and doubt will starve to death!

79

For Spiritual Endurance – Start Here

#1 – Simplify	Lay aside every weight and sin. Sin must be dealt with, that is, eliminated. Don't play around with sin, remove it immediately. God will take away our sin if you place your faith in Him. Distractions must go. Anything that produces a conflict with following Jesus must be abandoned.
#2 – Endure	We must run the race, never stop, never let up. Endurance is easier when you simplify. Following Jesus all the way means making disciples just as He did, doing Kingdom work He has called you to. It means embracing Jesus as our example.

How do we Simplify and Endure?
There are five things that you must do to simplify and endure and be part of a continual lifestyle following Jesus. In other words, you must continually engage in these five things.

Repent	Give up everything that keeps you from endurance. It starts with sin – complete and total repentance means you will no longer follow that way but follow Jesus. Repent also of attitudes, and the busyness of distractions that weigh you down.
Inventory	Take time to pray and discover everything you are doing that is unnecessary and hurting you spiritually. Ask the question: What am I doing that leads me to sin? Why am I doing this? Why does that seem important?
Eliminate	If you aren't willing to eliminate, you haven't really repented. Get rid of activities, attitudes and obligations that hurt and possessions that demand. This may seem difficult, but you can do it, especially once you make it your lifestyle.
Fortify	Do things that strengthen you spiritually. Start with the following: **PRAY, SPEND TIME IN THE BIBLE** and hide its word in your heart and finally fellowship with other followers of Jesus.
Reproduce	Simply help others through this process. Bring someone along and stay committed to the process.

You Are What You Eat!

The Action

- *Eating is a necessary response to a felt need.*

- *Second, eating and drinking only benefit you, when you eat and drink.*

- *You can't over eat when it comes to feeding on Jesus!*

- Are you satisfied with Christ alone?
- Do you feed on His death for you as your only hope of eternal life?
- Do you feed on Him daily in His Word as nourishment for your soul?
- Do you enjoy all that He is for you, both now and for eternity?
- If not, the answer is simple:

Change your Diet!
This is Step 1!

My Spiritual Diet Changes

Directions: Use this page to write your plan on how you will accomplish Step 1.

Step 2-Resign from Doing God's Job

"So then, just as you received Christ Jesus as Lord, continue to live your lives in Him, rooted and built up in Him, strengthened in the faith as you were taught, and overflowing with thankfulness." -
Colossians 2:6-7

Write your letter to God and turn in your resignation, here is an example.

Dear **GOD**,

OK, I resign. I've been trying to run the world and probably the universe, at least the things I thought I controlled and I'm fed up doing this job, it's too much. I've never been a quitter, but I quit. Please take the job back.

I know you won't do things the way I would've done it and I'm Ok with that, but I'm sure you will do a much better job. Please take it back! I need to be able to sleep at night and to just sit back and watch the great things you're going to do in my life. I know that you are in charge and that you'll take care of things. I know there will be days, when I want to take control but don't let me, remind me so I don't have to cry again because I tried to be you.

You are **PERFECT and know me better than I know myself!** You may not do it exactly when I want it, but you are always right on time. Take this as my final resignation. Thank you and I love you Lord!

I Resign !

Dr. Mel

My Spiritual Job Changes

Directions: Use this page to write your plan on how you will accomplish Step 2.

Step 3 – God Loves Order

This is where we stumble, things happen when He is the orchestrator of it.

16 "For God so [greatly] loved *and* dearly prized the **world, that He [even] gave** His [One and] [a]only begotten Son..." John 3:16

The Greek definition for **WORLD** is **COSMOS** which means Orderly Arrangements, Systems, & Its Inhabitants. This leads us to believe that He Himself **ALIGNED** the Universe, our land, our lives, and it all works! Everything exists to lift Him high.

GOD doesn't expect us to produce until we get things in order... **ARE YOU IN ALIGNMENT TODAY**? In your **MIND, FAMILY, CHURCH, JOB; THERE MUST BE ORDER IN EVERYTHING YOU DO!**

YOU MUST ALIGN YOURSELF WITH HIS WILL FOR YOU; IN ORDER FOR HIS GLORY TO SHOW UP IN YOUR LIFE.

Always
Let
In
God
Now!

Step 3 – God Loves Order

Take These Steps Towards Getting It Right:

1. **CREATE** an undying relationship with **GOD** (Personal and Intimate)

2. **CHANGE** your thoughts to match His thoughts about your life

3. **REARRANGE** your Priorities (God first, Family, Occupation)

4. **CHANGE** your **MIND** (**M**ain **I**ngredient **N**avigating your **D**estiny)

5. **FOLLOW HIM** who gave you power to trample over those things you call problems and issues

6. Be **A SERVANT** and have a **SERVANT's HEART**

7. Be **A GIVER** and not a **TAKER**

8. **CHANGE YOUR ATMOSPHERE** "Let your light shine." **Matthew 5:16**

This your opportunity to start today, but you must align it all, not just some things. Once you complete this step then you are ready for Step 4.

Straightening My Crooked Ways

Directions: Use this page to write your plan on how you will accomplish Step 3.

Step 4 – Have GOD FAITH

When you're in **ALIGNMENT** with the Father, you can **SPEAK** to things that **CAN'T TALK BACK**. You can tell that **PROBLEM, ISSUE, OBJECT, DISEASE**, etc., that it doesn't belong to You! Karen Clark Sheard song, states **MY WORDS HAVE POWER** and they do. So speak it into existence.

We need to **HAVE GOD FAITH**, because **HUMAN FAITH** is insufficient.   Change your mindset.   **Hebrews 11:3** says,*"that which is seen didn't come out of something physical"*. **WE NEED TO BE PEOPLE THAT RELEASE WORDS FILLED WITH FAITH.   THE TRUTH OF GOD IS HIGHER THAN REALITY**. Walking in **ALIGNMENT** gives you the **RIGHT** to see that **FAITH IS NOW**!!!

FAITH converts your humanity into divinity.   Remember, Philippians 4:9 – *"I can do all things through Christ which strengthen me."*   The reason the enemy (**E**very **N**emesis **E**ntering **M**y **Y**ard) doesn't want you to clean up your speaking is he wants to keep you in the present.

Are we truly walking in ALIGNMENT with GOD?
Is your "VERTICAL" lined up with your "HORIZONTAL"?

Vertical	Your Relationship with God
Horizontal	Your Relationship with People

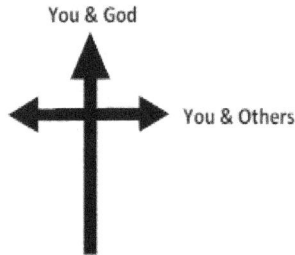

You & God

You & Others

88

My Spiritual Faith Walk

Directions: Use this page to write your plan on how you will accomplish Step 4.

Step 5 – Who Am I In Christ?

I AM.

Confess these with your mouth.

• **I am** an expression of the life of Christ because He is my life.	Col. 3:4
• **I am** chosen of God, holy and dearly loved.	Col. 3:12
• **I am** a son of light and not of darkness.	I Thess. 5:5
• **I am** a member of a chosen race, royal priesthood, a holy nation…	I Pet. 2:9-10
• **I am** an enemy of the devil.	I Pet. 2:11
• **I am** anointed by God.	I John 2:27
• **I am** loved.	I John 4:10
• **I am** like Christ.	I John 4:10
• **I am** the salt of the earth.	Matt. 5:13
• **I am** the light of the world.	Matt. 5:14
• **I am** commissioned to make disciples.	Matt. 28:19-20
• **I am** Christ's Friend.	John 15:3
• **I am** chosen and appointed by Christ to bear fruit.	John 15:16
• **I am** free from sin and enslaved to God.	Rom. 6:22
• **I am** a new creation.	II Cor. 5:17
• **I am** given strength in exchange for weakness.	II Cor. 12:10
• **I am** a son of God and one in Christ.	Gal. 3:26,28
• **I am** Abraham's seed…and heir of the promise.	Gal. 3:29
• **I am** a saint.	Eph. 1:1
• **I am** a fellow citizen with the rest of God's family.	Eph. 2:19
• **I am** righteous and holy.	Eph. 2:24
• **I am** capable.	Phil. 4:13

My Spiritual Awakening

Directions: Use this page to write your plan on how you will accomplish Step 5.

Step 6 – Living & Applying The Word
THE WORD IS POWER!

There are things that we must do to Live and Apply the word to our lives. Here are few things that you can apply to your daily living as you spend more time with God.

Important: Read the Word (the bible)

Read the WORD: Study it by reading and writing it down, get to know Him who created you and understand His purpose for your life. Devote time to prayer and constantly study God's Word. Hear what He has for you.

Memorize: It's impossible to apply the word if we can't remember it, especially if we're going to "hide" the Word in our hearts. Memorize the scriptures it will strengthen you and will be continual food to your soul, especially when you're not able to read your bible. In order to penetrate the heart and soul we must "lay up the words of His in our heart and in our soul" (Deut. 11:18, KJV). Get in the habit of memorizing some scriptures each day.

Meditate: I read a book by Writer and philosopher Edmund Burke he mentioned, *"To read without reflecting is like eating without digesting."* This tells me we must ingest God's Word. In the parable of the four soils (Matthew 13:3-9; cf. 18-23), Jesus tells of a sower who goes out to sow seed in his field, only to find that some seeds – the Word of God (Matthew 13:19) – had fallen on "rocky ground, where they didn't have much soil, and immediately they sprang up, since they had no depth of soil, but when the sun rose they were scorched. And since they had no root, they withered away" (13:5-6). Don't be a person with no root.

My Spiritual Application Plan

Directions: Use this page to write your plan on how you will accomplish Step 6.

Step 7 – Sowing

What is sowing? Do we truly understand the concept of it?

GOD GIVES US THINGS TO SHARE; GOD DOESN'T GIVE US THINGS TO HOLD.
MOTHER TERESA

God loves sowing and there are many ways to sow. The bible clearly talks about how we are God's field and God's building.   The kingdom will never be here on earth without this principle being carried out.

In **Galatians 6:7** (AMP), His word states, *"Do not be deceived, God is not mocked [He will not allow Himself to be ridiculed, nor treated with contempt nor allow His precepts to be scornfully set aside]; for whatever a man sows, this and this only is what he will reap."*

Charles Stanley mentioned in his teaching, that there are some principles about sowing:

1. **The principles apply to believers and non-believers** – remember we all will go to the throne to plead our case before Him
2. **You reap what you sow** (this means anything you sow) – Be careful here because if you sow negativity you will not get positivity
3. **We reap more than we sow** – A single seed can produce thousands
4. **We reap later than we sow** – don't look for an immediate seed, it takes time to produce, keep working with it.

My Spiritual Seed Plan

Directions: Use this page to write your plan on how you will accomplish Step 7.

Step 8 – Nurture the Seed

You are the heir to the Kingdom and God needs you to take care of what He has placed in your hand. This is when elevation in the things of God comes. I had the opportunity to read a story about a CEO that made caring for a seed and teaching integrity the best concept we can use in the things of GOD. Read the story below and meditate on the seeds God has given you and then ask yourself questions.

Here's the story,

"A successful CEO was getting up in age and decided to step down and needed to choose a successor. Instead of choosing those that were in his top management team he decided to choose from his young executive pool. He held a meeting to announce the decision but gave the young executives an assignment and time to accomplish it.

He gave each young executive a seed and alerted them this is a special seed. He advised them to plant it, water it and come back in a year with what they had grown. There was one that was extremely excited about the seed and was so eager to tell his spouse when he got home. He planted the seed, watered it, talked to it and did all he could with that seed, but it wouldn't grow. He grew weary and upset and even thought to go buy another seed and present it, but he didn't. He continued to nurture the seed that was given to him.

After a year went by the CEO called all the executives into the office to announce the next CEO. He saw all the wonderful trees and plants that were in the room but noticed one guy with an empty pot. He called the guy up to the front, the guy felt awful because he had nothing in his pot. The CEO made an announcement. He said, "this is your new CEO". Why did he make him the new CEO? People were shocked at the announcement.

Step 8 – Nurture the Seed, con't

Then the CEO said, "One year ago today, I gave everyone in this room a seed. I told you to take the seed, plant it, water it, and bring it back to me today. But he gave them all boiled seeds; which were already dead – it wasn't possible for them to grow.

He continued to speak, "All of you, except Jim, have brought me trees, plants and flowers. When you found that the seed wouldn't grow, you substituted another seed for the one I gave you. Jim was the only one with the courage and honesty to bring me a pot with my seed in it. Therefore, he is the one who will be the new Chief Executive Officer!"

- If you plant honesty, you will reap trust
- If you plant goodness, you will reap friends
- If you plant humility, you will reap greatness
- If you plant perseverance, you will reap contentment
- If you plant consideration, you will reap perspective
- If you plant hard work, you will reap success
- If you plant forgiveness, you will reap reconciliation
- If you plant faith in God, you will reap a harvest

Be careful what you plant now; it will determine what you will reap later. This story is for all of us that God has given seed to.

- What are you doing with your seed?
- Are you sitting on the seed?
- Are you planting it in bad soil?
- Are you substituting the seed He gave you for something else and aren't prosperous in it?

Think about it!

Step 8 – Nurture the Seed, con't

The seed God has given me is to tell the people of His goodness and how He brought me through. I pray that you see that I've done that in this book.

I'm not ashamed of the things He's given me and allowed me to experience, whether small or large. I'm grateful that He made me, Dr. Mel, the person she is, through the good and the bad. Everything I went through in life was for someone else. This explains the bumps in my life, but it was only a setup by my Lord and Savior Jesus Christ. He made me a living example.

God Bless!

My Spiritual Plan to Nurture My Seed

Directions: Use this page to write your plan on how you will accomplish Step 8.

I truly believe that I'm fulfilling my calling, especially since I see the evidence in my work in Ministry, Corporate America and teaching. I see the fruit of making a difference in the world. It just takes a few people at a time. I want to display the truth about my savior in every aspect I do.

Look at the diagram below, this data was pulled from Watson Analytics from some training that I delivered for a mass group of people in Corporate America. The larger the word the more you were commented about.

"This is awesome God! Thank you for the opportunity to let me serve you!"

Be Blessed!

Dr. Mel

I want you to be free and walk in your calling. God has chosen you for a reason. It doesn't take much to do it, it just takes effort to begin.

Contact us we'd love to hear from you.
Free Women of God Ministries, Inc.
at mybumpshaveapurpose@gmail.com or on Facebook at
Melanie P Manor.

Please include your testimonies and praise reports when you
write.

FREE WOMEN OF GOD MINISTRIES

835 E. Lamar Blvd., Ste. 348
Arlington, Texas 76011

Check out our website
for additional materials

mybumpshaveapurpos3.wixsite.com/mysite

www.ingramcontent.com/pod-product-compliance
Lightning Source LLC
Chambersburg PA
CBHW032047040426
42449CB00007B/1021